My Sister Is My Friend

WRITTEN BY
Hannah Markley

ILLUSTRATED BY
Larry Johnson

HARCOURT BRACE & COMPANY

Orlando   Atlanta   Austin   Boston   San Francisco   Chicago   Dallas   New York
Toronto   London

My sister finds my socks.

My sister finds my shoes.

My sister finds my book.

My sister finds my coat.

My sister finds my snake.

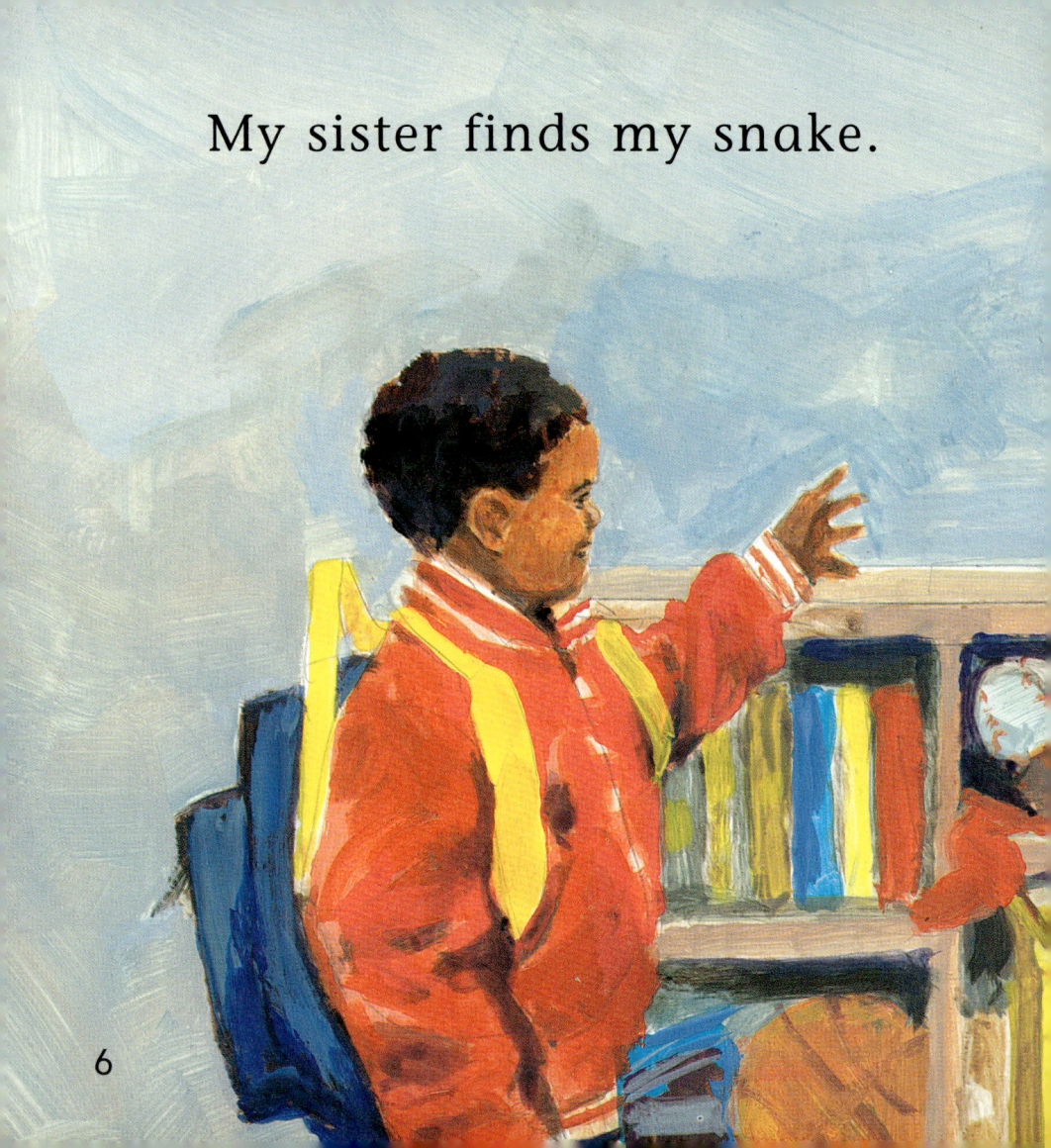

7

I'm glad my sister is my friend.